# fourteen poems

*Issue 3*

First published in 2020.
fourteenpoems.com

Designed and typeset by Stromberg Design.
strombergdesign.co.uk

Printed by Print2Demand Ltd, Westoning, Bedfordshire, UK.

ISBN: 978-1-910693-58-2

Hello and welcome to the latest issue of *fourteen poems*, the journal dedicated to celebrating the best in New Queer Poetry.

As always, we've chosen 14 of the world's most exciting queer poets, showcasing the diversity of the LGBTQ+ experience. This is the first issue solely made up of poems submitted during the global pandemic.

Read the whole book in one or dip in and out when you need a break from the world; *fourteen poems* is designed to make poetry accessible and relevant to you.

I usually resist trying to frame any work as the quintessential poem of a period (although Jericho Brown's "Say Thank You Say I'm Sorry" comes pretty close), but there are definite themes apparent in many of these poems: isolation and the need for connection, the quiet peace of intimacy, the longing for release, grief. As queer people, we often experience these feelings in our everyday lives, but the pandemic has magnified them for many of us. If you're feeling stressed or confused by everything, I hope we can offer a little respite.

Stay safe!

**Ben Townley-Canning**
Editor

Instagram: @14poems
Twitter: @fourteenpoems

# contents:

**Travis Tate** is a queer, Black playwright, poet and performer from Austin, Texas. Their poetry has appeared in *Borderlands*: *Texas Poetry Review, Underblong, Mr. Ma'am, apt*, and *Cosmonaut Avenue*, among other journals. *Maiden*, their debut poetry collection, is available from V.A. Press. They earned an MFA from the Michener Center for Writers.

You can find more about them at travisltate.com

## The Night is a Museum

This is our night, the intimate made apparent like the sea
pounding its pretty little head against the sand, creeping
through your toes. This night caught, not empty, filled to
the brim with expectations. Our lives placed upon a tight
rack of desired meats. Night, like a fissure in the plain
black sky, a comet bringing on some kind of magic that
we both arch our backs to. This is ours, the bonded sweat,
the kiss on the shoulderblade, the arm asleep for most of
the night under the body, like a temple to something that
is holy, washed in heaven, the minute you open your eyes
to me in the morning, cascading through the window near
the bed. Our night has left us, but we are together.

**Travis Tate**

**Ella Duffy**'s debut pamphlet, *New Hunger*, was published by Smith|Doorstop in May 2020. Her work has appeared in *The Rialto*, *Ambit*, *The North*, *bath magg*, the *Guardian*, and more. Her second pamphlet, *Rootstalk*, was published by Hazel Press in November 2020.

Instagram: @elladuffypoet
Twitter: @Els_Duffy

## Two women sit for breakfast

comfortably quiet. Between them,
something will move; steam from the oats,
or light, painting a bowl of plums.

Whatever was promised last night can wait
until the table's clear
of honey-licked spoons and crumbs.

There are so many ways to be gentle.

Outside, the morning turns to its clouds,
but for them, the hour threads itself golden.
Let them sit a while longer;
there are always oranges to peel.

I'd like to know how many years we'll have.

**Ella Duffy**

**Padraig Regan** is the author of two poetry pamphlets: *Delicious* (Lifeboat, 2016) and *Who Seemed Alive & Altogether Real* (Emma Press, 2017).

Instagram: @padraig_regan
Twitter: @padraig_regan

\* *Katsu ika odori-don, which translates as 'dancing squid rice bowl' is a dish of fresh squid served on rice. The squid is so fresh, in fact, that its muscles are seen to twitch or 'dance' in reaction to sodium.*

## Katsu Ika Odori-don *

I know what animates this bunch of tentacles:
it's just the salt in the soy filling the blanks in the dead nerves.

I tell myself this, but as the GIF keeps looping
through the same few frames, the same pattern of flicks & wiggles,

it's difficult to not imagine necromancy, or worse,
the dumb protest of a lump of brain-stem.

At any moment I could stop this wonky, eight-limbed Charleston,
not by eating it but by closing the tab. I tell myself this.

Is it empathy that's stopping me, a sense of duty
to bear witness & attend to the whims of the dead,

no matter how random? Not quite. Maybe it's envy
or aspiration that keeps me watching. But do I envy

the hand that pours the sauce & turns this stump of a squid
into its own erratic puppet, or aspire to be as pliable

as the clump of tissue that receives its grace?
If, as the physician says, the soul weighs twenty-one grams,

it seems important that we find a way
to figure out how much of this is sodium

& therefore how much of us is lost in a fit of crying,
or passed back & forth throughout a night of sex.

It will take perhaps a minute for the last shudders
to peter out & the tentacles to lie still again.

I want to know is it best to wait before you start
the process of dismantling the legs with your chopsticks

& testing each one for its flavour; or is the reciprocity
of your tongue's movements part of the pleasure of the dish?

When the time comes, feel free to keep a limb of mine
& drench it with soy if you feel lonely.


**Padraig Regan**

**Juniper Yun** is a South Korean born, Oakland-based interdisciplinary visual artist and writer. Her work explores themes of identity, desire and transformation. She has showcased her visual and spoken work in several exhibitions and galleries nationally and internationally. In 2018, she published her first poetry booklet, *Conversations of Water*, through Papeachu Press, and completed a writer's residency through RADAR Productions in line with the San Francisco Public Library in 2019. Because of her experiences as a multi-racial, transgender woman of colour, Juniper utilises her passions in art-making and cultural studies to empower her communities. Juniper currently works as Program Associate for The Transgender District in San Francisco, the world's first legally recognised district dedicated to those of the transgender experience.

Instagram: @tigerrabittiger

*(for my father)*
Sticky skin draping as gossamer over your
skeleton where my two hands discover
infinite textures in finite moments.
Your hands which are in mine are melting
as if light into night sky, like the ice I feed you
hour per hour. Your freckled, worn gossamer blueing
against my blood flushed skin tearing pink,
tears mimic shooting stars which are just dead things
evacuating space to find a place of rest.
Finally, finally, you say as I close my book,
as we close your book.

## Origin

*(for my mother)*
Chili peppers stain our nailbeds the
color of summer, my nose runs from the scent
trapped in the bridge of memory. The sun
bounces off your baldness and creates a moon
in the form of a mother. Your back so small, your
shambling moves me more than my own
legs, which were once yours, which are always
yours. You, yours, us, running from memory
but in circles, always towards you, with these
legs that aren't mine but are ours, that are gifts,
that are roots that refused to root.

**Juniper Yun**

**Kendrick Loo** is the reviews editor for *Singapore Unbound*. His poetry and literary reviews have been published in *Tayo Literary, Empty Mirror* and *The West Review*, among others.

Instagram/Twitter: @stagpoetics

## Bildungsroman with Thorns

He told me he had gutted a chicken
trekked through the mud
              until it was too dark to see
        asked if I had seen the trees
              how they grew

                              trunks
                          littered with thorns
        He said they hurt someone
a guy tumbled        skin forced onto spikes
        talked about tears                how the medic spent hours
        cutting cloth        the welling of blood
                              a bright emergency
I found out the tree's name later
                    *bombax ceiba*
        Surely something about it
                    related to paradise
How boys were sent to be kissed        by thorns
        in promise of        manhood
              What is strength but bodies
                              shaped by stimuli
        root hairs inching
                    for water        branches
                                        for light
When he spoke of paradise
        I thought of childhood                How I woke
                              with bruises on my knees
There are pains I use    for my living
              or am used to biting through
                        but even the toughest of us
                              want to be loved
It is what we shine a light on that tells us
        *This is a paradise        I can understand and keep*

**Kendrick Loo**

**Erin Jin Mei O'Malley** is a queer Asian American writer. Their work appears or is forthcoming in *Redivider, wildness, Tinderbox Poetry Journal, Cosmonauts Avenue,* and others. They have received a scholarship from the Lambda Literary Foundation and nominations for a Pushcart Prize and Best of the Net.

Twitter/Instagram: @ebxydreambxy

## Ode to Moshing at Bikini Kill's First Show in 20 Years

at any other concert, it begins / with a trilogy of imitation: some girl's / old driver's license, my silver chain, real enough / only to rust, & my full moon / cheeks searching the night / for shadows, angles at which I can un/become a girl / I look nothing like, ends / with at least one of these fakes fooling someone. / but at least I get in the door. I'm there / until the encore or / a boy or girl mistakes me for a boy or girl, / the venue locking up or the welt of someone's fatal language, whichever is first to kick me out. violence / is never the answer but somehow always / the choke-blue question / that pretends it's better to ask for anatomy than permission / or forgiveness. at any other concert, it's the song all the bruiseless throats sing / along to. but I'm here & it's tonight & it's never / been tonight before. the stage lights go down, turning the volume of the voices in the pitch- / black room the fuck up. bikini kill starts playing "rebel girl", & I scream, feel / the lyrics / rip from my vocal chords. my mother / calls this genre of music brutality, I call it reunion. this / is how I raise my voice / from the dead. each time / someone stage dives into the river of riot / grrrls, we chant a moat of sound around us. we wall / of death ourselves, crowding the room / with our afterlife, the one where we are most safe / slamming our bodies into themselves / until they become our own, when we shed the terminology of our pasts / like old blood / cells. the first time I ever moshed was in a stranger's / backyard. I pushed myself into the gravel / of what I would call a song & / what my mother would call a cry / for help, & a certain myth of that night / says we moshed so hard we shook / the peaches from their trees. some would call the way we crushed / the ripe fruit beneath / our combat boots a tragedy, but we / know how any sweet thing with a pit will bruise. man / was made mortal, but we are not / men. we retell our genesis beginning / with death. call it legend or remix, how our graves / are meant only for the names we've chosen / to bury. when my body falls, let it / fall where it may: the soil was made soft / just for us.

**Erin Jin Mei O'Malley**

**Jade Mutyora** is a Black mixed-race, queer writer living in Yorkshire, focusing on writing poetry, fiction and creative nonfiction. She is currently working on two novels for young people.

Twitter: @jademutyora
Instagram: @jademutyorawriter

## Worship

Because the glaring streetlamp's reflection

catches each strand of your halo in a different way

and the room that would be ordinary

if it weren't for the offerings of its altar

becomes a cathedral when it frames you


Heaven is reachable with soaked fingertips

ludicrous rituals take on grave solemnity

glossolalia is the password to enlightenment

dissolving foundations of logic so that

even an atheist, a heretic, a witch

believes

**Jade Mutyora**

**Kevin Bertolero** is the founding editor of Ghost City Press and is the author of four collections of poetry, most recently *Love Poems* (Bottlecap Press, 2020). His nonfiction book on gay cinema is forthcoming in 2021 with Another New Calligraphy. He is currently studying in the MFA program at New England College.

Instagram/Twitter: @KevinBertolero

## From Cinnabar Basin

Halfway through
*City and the Pillar*
when the storm rolls
in we look to the top
of Electric Peak, sheep
herd on the mountain-
side, hunted by the grey
wolves of southern MT
& on Palmer Mountain to
the east across Yellow-
stone River we see the
switchbacks & the mount-
ains & rivers without end
just like the poet said &
palm to palm is holy
palmers' kiss you say
but we are not saints, we
are fags & cannot let
lips do what hands do so
we wait for the storm
to pass & then lay down
in the cold night grass &
just pray & pray to see
big sky   clear   w/ all
those shooting stars.

**Kevin Bertolero**

**Brad Beau Cohen**'s poetry has been anthologised twice by Fincham Press, exhibited in The Hilbert Raum and SomosArt House, and published worldwide by Elska magazine. His erotica ebook *Outside These Lines* (Berlinable) was an Amazon bestseller. Cohen is based in London and currently working on his debut pamphlet.

More information can be found on his website bradcohen.co.uk

## Sugar Water

Boys never stay
to taste the seasoned skin
it's a treasure to be saved
for when wicks are waxless
& smoke floats tidal

let the room of ghosts watch
your taking of stock
tally with the tongue
whispered 'fuck's wrapped
around knuckles

with curl ribbons of left breath
la petite mort &
borrowed cologne
wilting on your lips
like a stone-side bouquet

find the jewel in your belly button
a molten mother-of-pearl
then taste that sugar water
biology of both
& anoint your cupid's bow

map uncharted hip riches
edgings of seminal lace
veins of gold on your bruised ass
& when your smile bankrupts the moon
know you gave yourself these gifts

**Brad Beau Cohen**

**Clayre Benzadón** is an MFA student at the University of Miami, editor of *Sinking City*, and Broadsided Press's Instagram editor. Her chapbook, *Liminal Zenith*, was published by SurVision Books. She was awarded the 2019 Alfred Boas Poetry Prize for *Linguistic Rewilding* and has recently been nominated for a 2020 Best of the Net Poetry Award for *Pink Moon*. Additionally, her work has been featured in places including *Pussy Magic, Kissing Dynamite* and *Hobart*, and is forthcoming in *ANMLY, Fairy Tale Review*, and *Crêpe and Penn*.

Instagram/Twitter: @clayrebenz

## Radish

I hide my face in the dish
of radishes you put out
for me. You tell me

it means famine,
my name. Fine,
I understand

that according to Chinese
philosophy, the fingers
of a woman are sometimes

called scallions,
but when you poke
me, it is like shards

of root fuchsia, you
turn me hot with color,
with rashes on my cheeks.

The companion plants
mop pain up like onions
so I stung my eyes

with the garnish tips.
Girl, you are a diva
and clever,

freedom tiger,
and babe, and babe and

bunny tail and cherry
belles,

I'm about to dash over
and form the reddest
reef of holy (less vulgar

than the Greeks)
and invigorate your
navel with the damn

invitation. Sweet spring
god, you are an offering,
you leaned into me,

sprouted two inches off
the ground, sharp,
racing, racy.

I had to sow you
in first frost,
beautiful. You

are worth the weight,
leaden and quickly
appearing.

**Clayre Benzadón**

**Ellora Sutton**, 23, is a queer poet from Hampshire. Her work has been published by Young Poets Network, *Poetry Birmingham Literary Review* and *Mookychick*, among others. She won the inaugural Artlyst Art to Poetry Award and the 2019 Pre-Raphaelite Society Poetry Competition. Her debut chapbook, *All the Shades of Grief,* is out now from Nightingale & Sparrow.

Twitter: @ellora_sutton

## Moonshot

Pork chow mein in the park,
the meat red-lipped, girlish.
My new dress is ruined
with sticky red sauce
in the shape of an iris.

She looks at me
and I have the tiny yet full body of a starling
the size of a whole heart
beating rapidly. I am bones
blue as Heaven in her tinfoil carton.

I read somewhere once
that this planet can only withstand
five more atomic bombs
and this, surely, must be one of them.

**Ellora Sutton**

**Gabrielle Johnson** lives in London and works in publishing. She writes psychological and sometimes magical fiction and poetry. Gabrielle is the co-founder and editor of *clavmag*, a digital literary magazine publishing creative writing by queer, trans and non-binary people. In 2019, they were selected as one of twelve emerging LGBT+ writers to participate in Spread the Word's creative writing workshop programme 'The Future is Back'. You can read their work in Cipher Press's chapbook, *There Will Always Be Nights Like This*.

Instagram/Twitter: @gabrielleMCJ

## When I help you write job applications
## on Google Docs from 300 miles away

your words are tripping in your mind as you write.
shoelaces undone, hands out,
yelling.
the cursor is blinking and i'm watching you,
three months ago
with your nose in the gorse,
eyes covered cause i'm shining too bright.
the yellow flower smells like coconut and
three months ago you made fingerprints
in my bones.

when you write job applications on Google Docs I watch your cursor move.
get stuck on the page thinking about the way
your feet glide on rocks
but slip on tarmac.
how your face is cleaner than vodka
when you come up from the water, nose first,
sucking in air and taking me with you,
into your lungs,
your stomach, your heart.
I'm dropping crumbs so I can find my way back.

this morning I woke up with the memory of your spine against my mouth,
shut off my alarm, wiped my lips clean,
reached for my laptop.
i'm dropping commas that say i need you,
cutting double words to tell you
come home.

**Gabrielle Johnson**

**Dante Micheaux** is author of *Amorous Shepherd* and *Circus*, which won the Four Quartets Prize from the Poetry Society of America and the T. S. Eliot Foundation. His other honours include the 2020 *Ambit Magazine* Poetry Prize, and fellowships from Cave Canem Foundation and *The New York Times* Foundation.

Instagram: @amorousshepherd
Twitter: @DanteMicheaux

## Black Boy as a Landscape

Night.

Outside, the elusive savannah
appears,

its trees dangling their tresses
in a shameless wind.

The calm betrays its lode
of lapis lazuli, carnelian

and volatile history—
married to eternal life.

How I long to ride its range:
high, dark and stretched

before me.

**Dante Micheaux**

**Kat Payne Ware** is a poet from Bristol, UEA Creative Writing MA graduate, and founder and editor of *SPOONFEED*, an online literary magazine for creative and experimental food writing. Her work has been published in various journals and magazines, most recently *Brixton Review of Books* and *Seiren*, and was commended in the 2020 Verve Poetry Festival competition.

Twitter: @katpayneware and @SPOONFEEDmag